War Baby Express

War Baby
Express

Roseann Lloyd

HOLY COW! PRESS
DULUTH, MINNESOTA 1996

ISBN 0-930100-68-9

Publisher's Address:

Holy Cow! Press
Post Office Box 3170
Mount Royal Station
Duluth, Minnesota 55803

This project is supported, in part, by a grant from the Literature Program of the National Endowment for the Arts in Washington, D.C., a Federal Agency, The Jerome Foundation, and by generous individuals.

The author wishes to thank the editors and publishers who first published some of the poems in this book.

"Angles of Vision" published in the anthology *Writing Our Way Out of the Dark: Survivors of Family Violence*, Queen of Swords Press, 1995

"Not Even a Shadow on the Sidewalk" published in *She Who Was Lost Is Remembered: Healing Incest through Creativity*, anthology published by Seal Press, 1991 and reprinted in the book *Gossips, Gorgons, and Crones: The Fates of the Earth*, by Jane Caputi, Bear Press, 1993

"Norwegian Spring, 1962," "Singing the Passage to Somewhere Else" published in *The Origin of Tigers*, a Loft publication of the writings of Loft-McKnight Fellowship writers

"Norwegian Spring, 1962" published in *Earth's Daughters*, The Girlfriends Issue, Issue 43/44, 1994

"Tenderness" published in *Common Journeys*, Issue 2, 1994

"40 Caprices for the Ginkgo Tree" published in *Hurricane Alice*, excerpted, Volume 6, Number 1, Winter, 1989. Nominated for a Pushcart Prize

"Lessons from Space" published in *Minnesota Monthly*, Volume 21, Number 1, January, 1987 and reprinted in Margot Fortunato Galt's book *The Story in History: Writing Your Way into the American Experience*, Teachers and Writers Collaborative, 1992

"Lisa Talking: Summer Storm, 1983" published in *Minnesota Monthly*, August, 1990

"Too Much Give" published in *Loonfeather*, Spring/Summer, 1995

"The Mississippi in Spring" published in *Wrestling with Your Angels: A Spiritual Journey to Great Writing*, by Janet O. Hagberg, Adams Press, 1995

"Painted Canyon Rest Stop" published in *Sidewalks*, Number 8, Spring/Summer, 1995

"To Be Content with What Is Given" published in *Acorn Whistle*, May, 1995

For Karen Jeffords-Brown, again, gratitude

AUTHOR'S ACKNOWLEDGEMENTS

Books come into the world with the help of many hands.

I want to express appreciation to my family and my friends who have supported my writing in countless ways.

For helping this manuscript come into the world, I send heart-felt thanks to: Jill Breckenridge, Susan Cygnet, Norita Dittberner-Jax, Brigitte Frase, Birgitta Rönnmark Fowler, Phebe Hanson, Carolyn Holbrook-Montgomery, Judith Katz, Deborah Keenan, Alice Jane Lloyd, Jan Levinsohn Milner, Jim Moore, Joe and Nancy Paddock, Richard Solly, Sheila Thomsen, Kathleen Sullivan and Cary Waterman.

Special thanks to Mary McDunn, artist and collagist, for honoring the occasion of this book by making the retablo that graces the cover.

Gratitude to Jim Perlman, Holy Cow! Publisher for his encouragement and support of my artistic vision, his attention to detail, and his devoted commitment to literature in its many voices.

Last, I want to thank the institutions that gave me financial support during the time some of these poems were written: the Minnesota State Arts Board, The Loft, the Loft-McKnight Fellowships for Writers, and the Minnesota Department of Economic Security.

May the Blessings Be.

CONTENTS

ORIGINS: WAR BABY EXPRESS

for Deborah Keenan and Lucille Clifton

In the beginning, there were locusts singing,
a mother rocking her baby on the transcontinental train.
Strangers held her, said, *Isn't she the smartest little thing?*
Back home in the Ozarks, Grandpa sunned her on the glider swing.
How did I end up here, in the land-locked North,
in a rundown neighborhood, no front porch?
In the middle of the story, the wicked king ransacked
the girl's childhood, pillaged her sack
of doll babies, her soft pillows of breasts.
Her brother—left for lost in the forest.
Neither bread nor pebbles could guide their wild hearts then.
That's why I could fall for a man on a whim,
because of the shimmer of the opals
he placed in golden rings, with leaves of rose and gold.
Safety was located in danger, in motion.
That's why I could jettison
several households, pensions, cedar chests—
a carload of books was all that was left.
My cherrywood library desk was found
riding a houseboat in Puget Sound—
held steady by surf logs rescued from the shore.
I lost the memory even, the grounding I was searching for.
What's left, then, at the end of grief?
At the end of brothers, breasts, the names of trees?
I had expected to be left with nothing, not with this:
a voice that bears witness
to human pain—
voice steady as locusts, as ocean, as transcontinental train.

PART I ■ CLOUD OF WITNESSES

"... resistance, at root, must mean more than resistance against war. It is a resistance against all kinds of things that are like war... So perhaps, resistance means opposition to being invaded, occupied, assaulted and destroyed... The purpose of resistance, here, is to seek the healing of yourself in order to be able to see clearly."

—THICH NHAT HAHN

WAR: JANUARY 15, 1991

for my brother, Philip

there was no name for my brother—him & the other young men
who refused to go to war
by refusing to do anything at all—
refusing to work register take a bath
or even stay in one place—
hitchhiking to the Boundary Waters
the refuge of water and pines
then off to the commotion of New Orleans   San Francisco—
refusing to do much of anything
except get high—

perhaps you wouldn't call them protesters
those white & black young men—
getting high as a way of life
usually means you forget what time the demonstration starts
but they were protesting in their own way
the path of nihilism
the path of despair
they didn't know that protest could be a spiritual path
like that of the Buddhist monks in Vietnam
who poured gasoline all over their shaved bodies—
the American kids did it without the Buddhism
their only consolation from Asia
was the opium   which was a true and steady
consolation   for a while

perhaps you wouldn't call them protestors—
the ones who refused to go to war
some of the neighbors said my brother was a coward
the skin-heads who beat him senseless said he was a faggot
the psychologists said he was acting out because of the family
some in the family said he was going through his wild phase
his great-grandmother Minnie said he was a sweet sweet boy

but we still don't have a name
for all the young men who refused to go to war
by refusing to do
anything at all

a woman I used to know
I don't remember her name
remembers my brother asleep in my apartment
one summer afternoon: *you had a purple velvet
couch cover* she said *his hair was long
and curly   he was such
a beautiful boy*

war brings death to us all
to the ones on the street

to the ones in uniform   to the ones forced to kill
death to all of us   who see
the faces of the burned and bloody bodies
something in us dies

we will never get done missing them
how can they have another war   when we haven't even
gotten over the last one yet?

when someone dies when you're young   you don't know
how long time is
the time you're going to have
to miss them

ANGLES OF VISION

for Judith Lewis Herman, M.D.

*In any war story, but especially a true one, it's difficult to separate
what happened from what seemed to happen... The angles of
vision are skewed. When a booby trap explodes, you close your
eyes and duck and float outside yourself... The pictures get
jumbled; you tend to miss a lot. And then afterward, when you go
to tell about it, there is always that surreal seemingness, which
makes the story seem untrue, but which in fact represents the hard
and exact truth as it seemed.*

—TIM O'BRIEN

when I'm walking   it's
the movement that counts
thinking   whatever
flits across   my mind
the way   a cat tracks
each purple shadow
catching the grass
& when I'm walking
I let myself
think about the doctors
who thought   my symptoms
indicated a tumor
buried deep
inside my head   the
headaches   the tunnels
of dazzling light
the weeping
breasts   their hands
wrapped my chest
and legs in a blanket
of lead   a grasshopper's
thorax   I was held down
like when my father

was on top of me & my mind
couldn't skip around
they turned my head
by the chin
like a lover   positioning it
so they could see
what was wrong   with
their pinpoints
of invisible light

& when I'm walking
I can see those x-rays
they showed me
mainly what you see
is skull
a chalky shadow
something you think
you don't get
until you're dead & bone-
clean   dead & buried
like my brother
who got buried
the year before   his hair
was thick & curly
I never saw his skull
I felt dead then
I couldn't think
about death   couldn't say
the word *incest*
which was buried
with all my feelings
held down by my
thorax
of symptoms
headaches   blinded
vision   weeping
breast milk   no
connection to anything

not even my moon   my
husband's body
heavy & remote
& he strange as my
father   my brother's
gaunt hip-bones
graceful as a girl
walking through
my mind   all the days
I couldn't get up
off the couch

& when I'm walking
I can see the gone
days   those days
on the couch   we lived
in the mountains
then   my husband's sunlit
body   didn't want any part
of maniacal fathers
dying brothers   not any
part of the truth   I could
only see in the screen of
nightmares   glimpses
in the morning
light   it was then
I started walking
walking   the muddy
back roads   across
the floodplain & up through
the fat thistles of the purple
knapweed & up
even farther to the canyon
walking up to the
cedars & pines
up to the cold
streams & with each step
the headaches

receded   memories came
rushing in
like the cold water   like
the spring
floods   swelling
the valley floor

& when I'm walking I let
myself remember her—
that young woman with
downcast eyes
covered by the long
blond hair—the woman
I used to be & I
welcome the remembering
how I made her
say the words out loud
in plain English   without
the benefit of metaphor:
my father sexually
assaulted my body

my father beat
down his sons
my youngest brother
refused to fight in Asia
but he died from the
Asian flowers blooming
in his veins—
that's no metaphor   that is
the flower of addiction
what we thought was beauty
was really pain:
don't tell the secrets
death rhymes with incest
they're the family twins!
my father is a Gemini—
do you see how fast

my directness can slip away?
& when I'm walking I feel
directly all my
feelings that want to
slip away   the fear &
& sadness & shame
& the anger
that wanted to hide
my anger   at my brother's
death   all mixed up
with Vietnam & the war
& its poppies that
took him anyway   the death
anger all mixed up with my
body's anger
at my father's military
assaults   transferred
from the South Pacific
to the home & in
my grown-up mountain home
my husband's violent
silence & when I'm walking
I welcome the remembering
& I can see
that I don't feel dead
anymore   I can see
I have talked &
raged & cried & stormed
myself back to life
all the way back from
the numbness
from the death thought
that my brother's life = my
life   now I feel
my own blood flowing
through my veins

& when I'm walking

I'm walking life back
into my scared   stiff
body that always did
what it was told & when
I'm walking I can
even think about
all the dead weight
that kept me down
the thorax of
symptoms   the doctors'
bewilderment   the rules
& threats in the name of love
black-outs   numb hands
nightmares   hands & fists
& silence   & fear
of all of the above
& I'm not afraid any more
when I'm walking
I forgive the men the
violence their bodies
have expended on mine—
all their rage & grief—
I let them have
their lives & when I'm walking
I let myself have mine   I
let myself think
of my friends & my lover—
the men unafraid to look me
in the face   unafraid
to see the damage
my brothers
I have to keep moving
& there's no more
headaches   even in the city
I'm walking up the canyon
walking with my brother's
lovely hips   up through
the knapweed   up to

the purple lupine   the fringed
gentian   the scarlet gilia
& on up to the shooting stars
walking into my life   walking
up the canyon   I never
reach the end of

NOT EVEN A SHADOW ON THE SIDEWALK

for Susan

A woman on *Frontline* goes back to the house
where her father raped her—
she had to look at the bedroom again
to find what it was she was missing
There   she said   and the camera
did a close-up on the wall   *that gray wall*
that's where I went
when he came to my bed
That little child
is the part of me that's missing

I was jealous when I heard her talking
because I didn't go anywhere in particular
when my dad climbed on my bed
It's not that I can't remember where I went
I didn't go anywhere
I was just gone   exploded like the Bomb
Evaporated   Annihilated
There wasn't even a shadow left
on the sidewalk
to say   someone's missing

My symptoms developed   like the side-effects
of nuclear war—numb hands   missing hands
nerve ends shot   wheezing chest
damaged vision: staring at the white light
weak limbs reamed out
like the inside of a sewer pipe
aphasia   memory loss   splitting
headaches

Symptoms are a way to have feelings:
the body keeps on living

after annihilation
that is, something called "I"
kept living   but never understood what people meant
when they talked about self-esteem
when they said incest victims had low self-esteem

I had lots of esteem
I always got good grades
first grade gold stars   Phi Beta Kappa
I was a good piano player   diligent
a good worker   good lay   good mom
I was no dummy
I could see the accomplishments
I had esteem
What did it have to do with me?

If the *I* was a *me*   it didn't have a self
There was no scale on which to measure
low   medium   or high   self-esteem
There was no oak yardstick to measure   no shadow
on the sidewalk
someone   was missing

Some people call this condition *despair* and it was
Some people call it *abandonment* and it was that too
Some people call child abuse *murder of the soul*
I can see that is what
happened to me
All those labels make sense to my mind
but what it was   as I experienced it
was simply
non-being

Drinking gave life to the ashes   to the body
of a self that wasn't there
When I was drinking I was there
I felt real
I could feel my hands

I could talk from the heart
I knew the me
who was drinking

But in the morning   it was back to   nothing
Back to wondering what to do
with myself   wondering   whether to make this choice
over any other   why this husband   or that lover
why   this job   no job   when would it be right to
go back to school   I was ready to leave for Canada
at the drop of a hat   everything I owned
in a backpack like Thoreau said   etc. etc.
I did the laundry   cleaned the bathroom   said *Who cares*

it's all an illusion   all Maya
I got that word from reading Strindberg
and he got it from the Hindus
life is an illusion
life is the dream that's dreaming us
That was my comfort   for nothingness
I was smart   ·
I could do lots of things
I had time   all the time in the world

I thought this was sophisticated
I thought my drinking was sophisticated
After all   my favorite toast
was the skoal Bente and I used to say

Guttår min sjel fukta din aska

which means in English   *Here's to you   my soul*
wet your ashes   I didn't feel the despair of
these words   I had not yet let
that terrible sense of abandonment   sweep over me
I didn't even know   my soul
was missing

I didn't yet   know
that there wasn't even a shadow
on the sidewalk

to announce my missing name

CLOUD OF WITNESSES, ALL SAINTS DAY

for the 18 Minnesota women who were murdered by their partners in
1989 and the 27 women who were murdered in 1990, and for their
children

1

Thanksgiving again, my daughter and I are coloring,
making shapes by tracing around our hands.

She is making a turkey, her fingers are feathers now,
bright and brown, burnt sienna, maize, and umber.

I'm drawing rings on my fingers, emeralds and gold,
and when I start on the matching bracelet, I'm startled

to see my wrist so small on the cardboard,
looking like it belongs to a girl no older than 12.

How can it be mine, this woman no longer a girl?
I've put on weight, but I still have small bones.

2

His hands were even beefier than when we were married. Meathooks.
How did I ever manage to escape without any broken bones?

The question was: *Could we talk about our daughter's health*
with a third party present?

When she's at your house, I said,
is she getting beat up?   Has she seen you

hitting anyone else?
You sound like a battered wife, he said.

I said, *That's because I was one.*
Fear rose in my throat, red blotches spread across my neck.

His face was an odd combination of blankness and broken edges,
as though he'd been informed he had cancer of the brain.

He turned to face the therapist.
She never went in for x-rays.

The therapist asked me to relate one incident,
I picked the first time, the argument about keeping the dog.

Don't you see, he said, *I can't
apologize—I don't remember. I have no emotional content*

for what she's saying.
He seemed to have no memory of

the other therapists we went to, each one saying
Hitting a woman is never acceptable.

It's possible it's true, he said.
I was always on edge in those days.

3
He was always careful not to break my glasses.
Careful to hit me on the back of the head, to pound the fleshy

stomach, the uterus, the fat of my back.
Careful not to hit our daughter when she was snuggling on my lap.

Overweight means I don't feel vulnerable.
My wrists give me away.

The first time he hit me: Thanksgiving, 1971.
.The term *battered wives* first used in research: 1974.

He used to be so careful, in surgery, tying tiny sutures.
An expert, he knew how to leave no marks that show.

The drawing of my hand looks like it belongs to a 12-year-old,
playing dress-up. Rings on her fingers, bells on her toes.

It was a shock to feel the floorboards, wind knocked out of me.
Like a child, I thought, how can someone who loves me do this?

In *The Times Book Review,* Jean Stafford, in braids, frowns
like a troubled girl, her husband, a batterer, stern beside her.

When I left him, I moved in with another man for protection.
It was the only way I knew to handle my fear.

Now I'm ready at any moment to dial 911.
I wouldn't hesitate to take a knife to him without warning.

I've gained weight, but my bones are still small.
There's no fear in my body, I say, but the weight stays put.

I've never told anyone before—I can't
remember how he looks naked.

Our daughter didn't make plaster handprints in kindergarten.
I can see her hands, strong and sturdy even then.

The phrase *rule of thumb* comes from old English law—
wife-beating allowed if the stick's no bigger than his thumb.

When I told the story of how he beat me up, why, and how,
his face cracked like neglected plaster in an empty house.

I could never believe it was happening.
It was always a shock to be slammed sideways against a door.

He was careful not to break my glasses.
Bruises—raw umber—don't show on the back of the head.

They told me it was good that I'd left when she was three.
But the body never forgets, the body of the marriage.

A boy in the hospital named our daughter Lady of the Woods.
She fell in love with crafts, working with her hands.

She made collages out of leaves, burned flowers into leather.
I dreamed of blue and green hands floating along a red wall.

Sometimes life hangs on by a fragile thread.
When she got out of the hospital her face was the color of milk.

It's the forever of it that I can't get used to, Tess cried,
placing her black moon bracelet on our daughter's wrist.

For years I hated my Bride Doll. I was ashamed.
Now she sits in honor, in her Chinese gold Lounging Pajamas.

Another woman said to me only this week:
I dread Thanksgiving coming. I was in such danger in my marriage.

50% of murdered American women are killed by their own husbands.
How can their daughters continue on?

In 1971, I was too scared to leave, knowing
most women are not killed until they're on the run.

In 1976, they wouldn't give me a restraining order:
doctors don't jeopardize their careers, they said.

As I packed, he said, *you're lucky to be getting out alive.*
After that, whenever I left the house, I checked for cars, guns.

In 1981, my retinas detached themselves. The eye doctors
wanted to know how many times I'd been hit in the head.

Overweight means I don't feel vulnerable.
But my wrists give me away.

In 1988, a bill was proposed to the Minnesota Legislature:
if a man shoots his wife in Deer Season, it's a misdemeanor.

The body never forgets.
Fear travels with me, at daycare, in the parking ramps.

Yesterday a grandmother's bones were found in the river willows.
She was last seen at the Rosedale Mall, four months ago.

In the next town, a doctor shot his wife in the head.
She was holding her children by the hand, walking out the door.

Danger is everywhere but we know that Rosedale is not
where the worst danger lies.

It is difficult to determine the cause of death
when only the bones are found.

Our daughter wears bells, ankle bracelets, silver rings.
Her room, red and pink, with crystals and plants, her new life.

Her father can wander in his memory loss
as I do in mine. I know why I've forgotten his naked body.

Doctor, lawyer, white-collar thief ...
Why are educated men excused when they're offenders?

Life hangs by a fragile thread.
At any moment it can snap, like the wishbone on Thanksgiving.

When she got out of the hospital, we went to the Garden of Eden.
She bought perfume made of cucumbers and honeydew.

She is bringing her self back to life.
All the whys dissolve into mystery.

COUNTY MENTAL HEALTH CLINIC, 1976

So, the therapist said, turning to face
him in the padded easy chair, where he sprawled

in his inimitable fashion, arms relaxed on the arm rests,
legs open, stretched out into the center of the room

where he took up more of the available space than the other
two—the therapist and me. *So,* the therapist said again,

*she says she's ashamed of herself because she didn't leave you
after you repeatedly battered her.*

*But now that she's said this, here, to a third party,
you can be assured*

*that if you touch her again, she will
leave you for good. What I want you to do now is take off*

*your glasses, and let her hit you in the face.
Hit you anywhere she wants. Hit you as hard as she can.*

I couldn't tell if the therapist was serious.
But I could see my husband

could no more let me hit him
than he could admit that his beatings of me were wrong.

Nobody touches me, he said. He looked shocked
that another man would betray him in this manner.

I couldn't bear to look at his astounded face.
The muscles in my face tightened, set.

I was getting ready to walk away, take the baby, go.
I turned, looked out the window.

Watched a small bird fly from one bare gray tree
to another, the clouds and river and sky all flat gray

behind them. The soul of our marriage
has flown out of me, I thought. There it goes—

with a body, soft gray feathers, and wings—
and nothing I can do will bring it back.

When I looked back at the room,
the men were blurry through the steamy window,

I could see their mouths opening, closing,
but I couldn't follow the conversation any more.

3 A.M., MOON OVER THE LAKE, LIGHTING MY FACE AND PILLOW

for Cary Waterman

A woman is walking barefoot across the snow,
through the heavy firs. Her dress
torn and bloody, her hair
matted, her hands outstretched.

As she comes closer, I see
ropes dangling from her wrists,
bruises on her arms
bluer in the moonlight. In one hand

she carries the pomegranate,
its oval open
to the shining ruby seeds.

In the other hand, the flowers:
day lily of ancient gold,
blue flag, sprays
of sunlit wheat, the fragrant rose.

She comes and stands still before me,
her gray eyes clear.

I open my arms to her, cradle
in the curve of my left arm
the flowers, let her place the
blood red fruit
in the palm of my right hand.

She smiles, whispers, *This is all you need.*

PART II ■ TENDERNESS

"Doesn't everything die at last, and too soon?
Tell me, what is it you plan to do
with your one wild and precious life?"

—MARY OLIVER

SINGING THE PASSAGE TO SOMEWHERE ELSE

The locusts have no king, yet go they forth,
all of them, by bands.
—PROVERBS 30:27

1

Every August, we collected locusts.
Their tiny hands and feet
gripped the bark of the pear tree tight.
Fragile appendages, thin as strands of
peanut brittle, the same amber glow.
We worked them loose gently.
The trick was to get just one out whole.
Then hold it up to sunlight, see the world
through yellow, the rich
smoky topaz, blown-glass figurine.

2

Thirty years later, grown up now,
I traveled back home. Grandma
gripped my hand tight, pulled me
over to her chair. *They're mean to me here,*
Rosie, keep putting my hair up in a bun
but I don't want to die. She yanked at her hair,
letting the combs and hair pins
fall to the floor. *Medicine*
makes my head itch bad.
I hid the pins in the bottom drawer.
Brushed out her coarse, silky hair
which fanned its new-born whiteness
around her face, over
her shoulders, and down her back
like a mantle, an aura, silvery wings.

I stood and brushed her hair.
Couldn't see a single streak of the peppery gray
from her turkey farm days. No auburn sweep
of the wedding album. No swatch of burning red

that marked her girlhood, the red of fiery
sarcasm. Just white, pure white
surrounding her tiny face
which had also been clarified of its past
colors to become the gaunt, dark
face of any Old One—any gender, any race.
She's at once a stranger
and my darling, I realized I was thinking
as I brushed and brushed her silky hair.

And so I came to be watching
when a band of Old Ones passed by
in a royal procession there. Old woman
from the Ozark hills, whittling
a small oak doll. Humming
elder, dancing his cow bells
up and down the line. A grinning shuffler.
Someone hunched over in a gray, worn shawl.
Magnificent spirit from India, her
eight arms and maiden's face
reaching up to the sky. Another man
in patches of felt, singing the old *joik*
songs, mourning the dying reindeer.
Cat calls in the throat.
Coyotes in the hills.
Locusts in the dark green trees.

I didn't ask them what they wanted.
Could see they were waiting for her.
Could see she was already on her way to join them,
even though she held me tight
when I said it was time for me to go.
She was on her way to join them, to be free
of us—to be herself, her new, white hair
lifting her away.

3

I had to leave her then.
The screen-door was childhood, white wood, black screen.
Outside the heat was steaming yellow haze.
Ancient red bricks, the color of zinnias.
Three men in white stood under the trees, smoking.
The locusts singing the passage to somewhere else.
I stood stock-still in the middle of it all.
Felt the wind of death blow through me like a shell.
Saw the smoke rising into the trees.
The haze yellow above the city.

Nothing hurts as bad in August.
The purpose of living
is to become this beautiful.

LESSONS FROM SPACE

*for Christa McAuliffe, the social studies teacher who won the honor,
from 11,000 applicants, of being a civilian observer-participant on the
space shuttle and died in the Challenger explosion, January 28, 1986*

Astronaut is a foreigner in a silver suit
walking on the moon but *Teacher*
is our familiar—only one step
away from *Mother*, the first step out the door.
Teacher, we say, and we can see her hands again
covered with the chalky dust
of our own first grade. We can hear
her voice, insistent, explaining
why and *how to* as we print
with our fat red pencils—
lower-case s's
fill all the spaces between the sky-blue
dotted lines.

Now we are paying attention
to the front of the room where Ginny Lindstrom
is holding up an orange, representing earth
and Walter Locke is holding up a lemon,
representing moon. Stephanie Jones gets to hold
the flashlight, representing light.
Teacher, we say, *we don't get it.*
Just try, she always answers, *everything*
will be O.K., if you will only try.

Now she is mixing bright blue tempera
which we will apply—not too thickly—to our maps
of the seven seas which swirl
around our wobbly pears
of continents, whose names we must also
memorize. *You must learn*
all about the universe. Teacher is moving

about the room, her sleeves smudged and dusty
like everything else in here, even the solitary
plant that shoots its flat spikes up
in front of the chalkboard, which is
also swirling dusty white, like the Milky Way.

After lunch, we put our heads on our desks.
Teacher is reading. She explains the hard parts,
how it is possible in the story
for Harriet Tubman to be underground
and following the stars at the same time.
This is as inconceivable as death or the idea of space
having no end.

We turn away from knowledge
and admire our snowflakes, falling across
the glass. We folded white paper and cut them out
yesterday. Teacher says every snowflake
is unique, which means, unlike any other. Teacher
says each of us is a unique individual, special
unto ourselves. It is snowing now, for real.
We can't see the stars at the end of sky.

If Teacher goes away, who will teach us *how to*
and *why?*   How to cut out free-hand
hearts. How to find
the drinking gourd on a starless night.
What is burning in those smudge
pots in the orange groves?   What happens
to machines when it's freezing cold?
Why does the TV keep saying
blow-up, melt-down, O-Rings
out of round?   Why are they looking
for freedom up there
in the swirling clouds, in the sky-
blue sky?

NORWEGIAN SPRING, 1962

for Bente Helene Moen

We walked out to the end of the peninsula
to the pine trees on a rise
where we could lie down on the soft new grass,
half in the sun and still see
the sunlight off the water in the fjord.
The wind was blowing off the water,
dufting to us the early spring—salt, pine trees,
wild berries and then! the fragrance
of the homemade cherry wine.
It was light and clear, tinted pink
like the shells along the beach and we
sat and skoaled the spring.
Sang Bellman songs. The whole day
was light and clear. You'd been practicing Swedish
the long winter nights, sitting up to listen
to the radio from across the border,

and so the first poem you said out loud that day
was a Swedish one you loved,
ty min kära är framföre alla andra i detta landet
and then you went on from there
improvising variations on the poem in English,
my beloved's smile is like sun over the waters of Israel
the refreshing waters of Israel.
We ranged all over the world, quoting
our favorite writers: Emily Dickinson, Jack
Kerouac, Lord Byron, Tagore, Haldis
Moren Vesaas, Basho! How we could talk!
Translating back and forth. We knew hundreds
of lines by heart, the endless
rhythms, counterpoint to the ocean waves. We wanted
to take in all the wonder in the world, all

the ecstasy, all the tenderness. *Ömhet,*
you loved to say this soft word for tenderness, *ömhet.*
I loved to listen to you.
So strange to have loved something so much
and not to have known it was a calling.

We knew something was calling.
We knew the other girls were busy cleaning, baking,
hiking, shopping, kissing boys.
We were lying under the pine trees, reciting poetry!
Reciting poetry and drinking wine.
We didn't need anything else
to make us happy that day—it was all
so intertwined—the poems, the wind, the
first erotic smells of spring, our yearning
for the secrets of men and each other's
laughter, the pink aura the wine
wrapped us in.

I'm not drinking any more, Bente,
and I've learned how to live without ecstasy
every day. But the tenderness,
oh, yes, the tenderness. I have that now
and the poetry
is still calling and the trees
where I walk and hear your clear, light voice.
Tu lu lilla söt snut. I call back to you.
I think about how you would be now, had you chosen
to live your life. Somehow, though,
I believe your words still come through me
and when I say a poem out loud,
I see you walking, walking towards me
through the trees.

TENDERNESS

for Richard Solly

when they got all the tubes hooked up to you
& let us come into the room,
you held my hand like it was a life-

line, you couldn't stay awake
but you made yourself talk to ask us
will you stay here

until I fall asleep & your hand
told us you wanted to come back to earth
& when it was Jim's turn,

he held your hand
with both his hands, covered you, safe,
& when it was time for him to go

you startled yourself awake, your voice
hoarse from all the tubes down your throat,
you said, *I love you, Jim*

& he replied that he loved you & we cried
because it hurt you so much to talk
& you insisted on it anyway,

& I think I was crying, too,
for the tenderness
that exists between the two of you & then

many days passed and even weeks
you were in & out of Demerol, in & out of
the outer spaces where drugs take you

& I would come to see you
& you would be curled up drowsy
& then you would

open your eyes & recognize me
& smile & say something like
nice earrings & drift off

again for a while & then
you would wake up & try to talk
& I would say, *you don't have to talk*

& you would say, *mmmm* & then you would always say
it was so great to see all of you guys here
when I came out of surgery

& then I would say, *I know that,*
you don't have to talk, I'll sit here by you
while you sleep & if all of this sounds like

the kind of story you tell a child,
well, maybe it is coming out that way
because pain makes us vulnerable, like children,

but you weren't even cross
you were tender-hearted,
asking how I was & what did I do that day

& what did I have to eat
& then I would tell you, *split pea soup*
& grilled cheese & you would say

you could hardly wait to get out & then
I would say, *do you want to go get a hot fudge sundae*
when you're better

& you would nod & say, *mmmm I'm getting better*
& if Jim was there he would talk
about taking you for a drive to see the red maples

in the fall & you would say the same thing
mmmm I'm getting better
& then we would tell you again

that you didn't have to talk & entertain us
& you would close your eyes
& sleep & when you woke up sometimes

you would look at me for a long time
in that sweet fearless gazing
that brings us back from the amniotic world

to earth, where the first
shape is the human face: when we see
another's face, we learn what it is

to have a physical body, to be here
on the earth, this tenderness of
walking in the world, where

you now are walking, your hands busy
handling all the beautiful objects
of daily life: coffee cup,

newspaper, butter & toast,
car keys, checkbook,
your gold & silver pen

but while I'm still remembering the blur
of white days & tubes & your hoarse voice
I want to tell you

how your hand held onto mine like a life-line
& you said, *will you stay until I fall asleep*
& I sat there a long time

& felt close to you
peaceful in the white, still room
holding you to earth

THE FLOATING WORLD

Ukiyo ... living only for the moment

When I flew in to this week's school 20 miles from home
they told me I could use the Global Education Office

the Global Teacher looked to be my daughter's age
in black leggings   China shoes

stylish jacket from Japan   she showed me
the desk I could use said *My daughter was born*

in a village by the Floating Gardens in Mexico ...
I got my jacket at Global Village and I remembered me

at her age   in my paisley shirts & mini skirts
The buzz words were different then

we talked about Target I Schools   Moffat
The Open Classroom   Give Peace a Chance

Now there's talk of magnets   IEP's   ESL   cultural
diversity   but our purpose has been the same—

to love the children
to create a safe place for learning without shame

Today the third graders are writing chapter books
a new chapter of their journeys every day

some search for gold   some want
to save the cheetahs   others determined to find Amelia

and her airplane   somewhere in the blue Pacific
Where does my energy come from   to keep loving this

floating from school to school   from poem to poem?
I think of my friends from the days of hope and flowers

we thought we were the vanguard of change
Tony burned out in 8 years   no more pony tails   no more tipis

inside the school   he's installing solar systems in San Diego
Carol   the one who looked   cool in her woven skirts

made it to her pension   went back to her husband in Chicago
without ever coming out of the closet   Angelica

beautiful in the way of Country Western singers with her
thick Indian hair   leaning back with the green coke

bottle in one hand   cigarette in the other   Breakfast 1968
She lost all her teeth in her 30's   died of cancer

before she turned 50   The art teacher has flown off to the
Colorado plateaus after rumors of dealing drugs   her friend

dumped dead in a San Francisco suburb   wearing silk underpants
Bob used to say *When I'm dead, don't think of me dead*

think of me in the hall by my door, getting kids to class ...
But I do see him dead   all the same

like Joe's brother   killed in Ethiopia   by God knows who
perhaps those who didn't want anyone rescuing the Ethiopian Jews

perhaps the CIA   perhaps a pissed-off dealer
he was so young   like my brother in his upstairs room

in the house with the ripped out stairs   his ripped out veins—
life moves to death so fast   sometimes   with a jerk like the

Tilt-a-Whirl at the State Fair   One summer we escaped the city
went canoeing in the Boundary Waters

he went out at sundown   spun the canoe in all directions
to catch the light   the canoe was so light on the blue water

If only he could have loved it   enough
If only I could've loved one man and settled down   for life

If only it weren't so debilitating   the Twentieth Century
If only we could understand the mystery of loss

My husband said he'd rather die than talk about his pain
There are so many kinds of death   Our baby

conceived on my brother's birthday   floated
off to another world   to that blue line between life and death

like the horizon we see from the airplane window
there's just as much sky as there is water   floating

The first time I saw that line I was flying over the Atlantic
dreaming Bente was dead   and when we landed   it was true

Dear friend   I wanted to see you again   read Japanese poems
walk in the Norwegian pines with their old man's beard

Another friend   dead to my life   appeared again
not in a dream in the flesh   after 27 years   he just walked

into the airport   *I've flown over the Atlantic 14 times*
since I lost you   and the Pacific

In 1984 I was flying back to Japan from my father's funeral
changed planes in Beijing

I sat all night in the hotel drinking Mai-tais
festive with their chunks of tropical fruits

thinking about you
where in the world you could be   We never know

who we are going to get to keep   in our lives   who
will hold us forever in their hearts

The day he was in Beijing   I was probably driving
to a school   like the day I heard Bob was dead

I was driving to a school on the opposite side of the Cities
had to cross the Mississippi three times   to get there

I was working in kindergarten   the teacher   who was
energetically overdue for retirement   announced to me

*Naps are forbidden now   you know   we're supposed
to be working on our Learner Outcomes every minute*

*so we just take longer for milk
We don't call it naptime   we call it milk*

She was rocking in a rocking chair in the middle of the room
The children were stretched out and rolling around

goofily on the rug   some of them were humming   some arguing
in Spanish   the plants were leggy and overgrown   the hamsters

and the death news making my eyes run
Isn't this just heaven?   She continued she was so in the moment

with the spirits of her children   *Can you think of any place
you'd rather be?   To tell you the truth*   I said

no, I can't think of any place I'd rather be   If I were
in Beijing   Rio   Dar es Salaam   I'd be doing the same thing

the kids would be the same   and   even when I
wish my life had turned out otherwise   and even when I hear

news of death   Camilla Hall   fire-bombed by the L.A. cops
over 100,000 dead in Iraq and the U.S. government bragging

it doesn't do body counts any more   it is still true
when I walk into a classroom   I am in heaven

in the body   in the spirit   in another world   In fifth grade
today Bee wrote *The Story of Nava*

his favorite dessert   When he was little
he thought the white pearls floating in the liquidy sweetness

were frogs' eyes   He laughed   pleased with his mother tongue
Today the first graders couldn't guess

the riddle: *I am short and blue and female—Who am I?*
but they laughed when I declaimed

Equal rights for short blue people and they all
waved their hands wildly with the right answer to the riddle:

When I was in jail I received many letters
from children—Who am I?   Today the third graders were writing

their chapter called *The Blue Dream*   In Shannon's story
Whitney Houston led Sam through Africa to save the cheetahs

Kong's woman warrior blew in with a sword   pony tail   flip flops
a blue robe resplendent with stars   Amelia Earhart

appeared to guide Judi to her long-lost plane
Amelia became a part of me   she's dead

to others   but alive in me   I am completing
my global education   at ease   with the continuing presences

of the dead   their fine blue horizons
I am completing   my work   daydreaming

about airplanes   about my dream last night
making love in an astral bed   above my bed

In my blue dream   the gift my lover brought me
was a brocade satin box of yellow and green paisley

sitting on 4 tiny rounded feet as gold as the small patch
of new water in the frozen lake   I see driving home from school

The pussy willows have started to open   It's the season
for the wolves to mate   for the bears to give birth in their

caves   sleeping   Tonight I'll watch Kristi Yamaguchi
fly across the ice   jump into her whirling triple Salchow

landing on her feet every time   In the morning
when I wake up   wrapped in my blue quilts

I'll feel young
although it doesn't make any sense why

So much death to have lived through

BECOMING A WRITER

my brother   the artist   dead of an overdose at age 21

they opened the earth and put him in
his gravestone   a slab on my heart   my voice box
bolted shut

desperate to get death off my chest
the dreaded thought   *the end of our family*
I followed him into the grave

took notes
there was no stopping it   once it started
the rush of feelings   the insistent

search for truth   this day's
truth   the pleasure
of the black ink pen in my hands

family secrets spilled out of me
like so many missing socks
I no longer needed to mate

my brother reached out his hand
raised me up from the shabby couch
smiled his bad boy   rabbi   smile

*there's an empty place at the family table
the artist's place   you sit there now
you might as well enjoy it for me*

grass grew high around his grave
I walked out   into it
it was soft and green   tempting under my feet

the birch meadow had a yellow aura
Brother   I said   my voice
riding my breath with ease

O loosened tongue
O naked feet
O grave   that is a door

PART III ■ 40 CAPRICES FOR THE GINKGO TREE

"Some star or other went out, and you, thank you for
your book and year."

—JOHN ASHBERY

40 CAPRICES FOR THE GINKGO TREE

for Phebe Hanson on her 60th Birthday

1

When my marriage broke in two
I couldn't get outside
myself, outside the *what ifs* and
whys—I set out to walk
and thought *I need*
something absolutely
other. I looked up and saw
the ginkgo tree.

2

Now I walk and chant my mantra—
obsession falls away—
ginkgo tree, ginkgo tree.

3

They're tough city trees, beautiful
shade trees, thriving
in swamps, compacted city soil,
even in the northern climes.
Resistant to disease.

4

Look at the soft, green
leaves, shaped
like fans, bi-
lobal. The bark looks soft, too,
the color of pussy willow.

5

Like the fish *coelacanth*, the ginkgo
was once thought extinct, in the West,
but it was being tended all along

behind the walls
of the temples and monasteries of China—
kept alive
by the work of celibate monks,
long dead.

6

The Latin name *Ginkgo
Biloba* ... sounds like water, like wind
chimes, spring winds through the trees.

7

The leaves are silky,
striated,
like a sun-spray—in the summer—
they have the texture of sex, the yielding
silky private places, inside of
me, inside.

8

Sex is extinct.
This celibacy is
not a choice, rather,
a necessity. Having spent 25 years
in the land of reproduction,
it's time
to dream of
Chinese monasteries
where celibate monks
are tending ginkgo trees.

9

On the day the Rose Garden
was being put to bed for the winter,
bushes cut back and heaped
with maple leaves, Kathy
gleaned the roses, filled her house
with yellow, peach, blood red,

pink, white, burgundy, delicate
edges, and the smell!
There were too many for a funeral, enough
for a lover's bower and so she also
gathered the yellowing
ginkgo leaves, saying, *If you fold*
them together, they make a rose.
You can never have too many
roses.

10

Snow is falling in the temples of China.
Once sex was a sacred temple, I can remember,
a bower of roses, I entered
with delight.

11

I've turned over my sexuality
to the safe-keeping of the gods of China
and so, by God, has Phebe
who writes of a smiling fat Buddha
snuggling in her pink and golden bed.
Dear Friend! Sister Celibate!
You following Miss Paulson into Redeeming Spinsterhood
and me the ginkgo tree.

12

What was it like to be a monk
in China? To live inside
the circle of spiritual friendship?
Inside of celibacy? What led the monks
to revere the ginkgo tree? Was it
the silky surface of the leaves,
both male and female? The vague
sense of skin? Or was it something
else again? The way the branches
grow like spokes in a wheel,
a mandala for you to look

up through
to the sky?

13

Lucky for me this December is so warm—
wind blowing like October.
Coming back from the Grand Dairy
with a quart of milk, I see
a ginkgo leaf on the sidewalk.
Crisp yellow leaf!
Brother monks in China, looking out for me.

14

Curious about my mantra,
I pick up my book of Chinese poetry.
But I can find no ginkgoes, only
poems bewailing the poet's hang-over.
Yes, plum wine, I loved you
once, too. In those days, I didn't need
the distraction of walking
through the trees.

15

The ginkgo trees
are the oldest trees on the surface
of the earth. 250 million years old.
Maybe the monks
simply liked old age.

16

Ellen says her mother
who was an interesting, learned person
when she wasn't being psychotic
planted a ginkgo in their back yard
telling Ellen it was a symbol
for eternal life. I wonder
if that was her gesture
for survival, psychic and otherwise.

17

In some parts of Asia,
when you turn 60, you're allowed
to enter childhood again, to slip
from stately maturity, and the cares
of adulthood. I imagine elderly monks
frolicking naked in a meadow.
It's almost spring.

18

But it's 10 months into this sojourn and
I'm fed up with age and time. I walk
down to the lake to talk to the
naked, wind-blown trees:
*If I don't find a lover soon, I'm going to go
insane.* They're not worried. They know
I'm not even looking.

19

I thought it was only men, I continued,
*who go crazy from lack of sex. Does this
desperation, then, turn
me into a man?* The ginkgoes laugh
at my logic, sigh in the movement of
spring—the wind, the shoots, the loosening
of ice on the lake.

20

The moon
is always female
and so is the lobe of the leaf
of the ginkgo tree.

21

Talmud says in order to be happy
you must do three things:
have a child,
write a book,

plant a tree.
Nothing about a life-long lover,
a lover for your life
and nothing more.
Just three things:
child, book, tree.
That's it, I'm done.

22

Golden and rust
earrings in the shape of a fan—
this gift for my friend
who has finished
her book, written in the voice of a man.

23

I see the word *ginkgo* is gathering
meanings to itself: survival, love
of work, androgyny.

24

Entering the summer heat, the second year
of celibacy, I learn from Antiga
that I've never seen
female ginkgo trees—
they are forbidden in Minnesota,
their blossoms
said to be odiferous, objectionable
like rancid butter.

25

I walk down to the lake,
hot and sweaty, yet overwhelmed with gratitude
for the monks
who didn't ban the female trees.

26

I'm shy, embarrassed
to confess to my friends
I thought they were my sisters
but they're really my brothers!
How does it feel, I say, *to be without
your mates, to long
for your mates in China?*   How does it feel
to have been brought here
by those who discount the isolation
they're imposing on their own kind?
Lonely trees! Sweetly female, bi-
lobal leaves.

27

Now I understand why
I didn't recognize the picture
in the encyclopedia, a ginkgo in full flower,
full and lacy, *also known as
The Maidenhair Tree.*

28

The next entry after GINKGO
is GINSBERG, ALLEN (1926-   ), author
of *Howl* (1955). I wonder what Allen Ginsberg thinks
about being on this page
with the words: *males are desirable
ornamentals.*

29

*It's a good thing the female
ginkgoes aren't allowed in Minnesota,*
says the clean-cut blond science teacher
holding forth
in the teachers' lounge. *They're messy,
not only smelly—
messy. They drop
all of their leaves at once.*

30

Have you seen the leaves?
Lovely, bi-lobal, fan-
shaped leaves. The softest green.
I, too, have been transplanted,
but do not know which country to long for.

31

Maybe they're content, my brother trees,
content now, without their lovers.
Maybe they love the seasons, the geese,
the endless clouds, the coming snow
that will soon nestle in their arms.

32

Talmud is correct.
It is possible to be happy
without sex, for the desperation
to be lifted. I've raised
a child, written a book,
and planted trees. Birch Trees.
Russian Olive Trees. Pine Trees.
In the gardens, with the roses,
the rhubarb, purple beans, snow
peas, lunaria, salsify root, the oyster
plant. I've planted many gardens.
Every house I've lived in—
I've left behind
trees and perennials,
something permanent, something
that stays.

33

Wide awake, at 5 a.m.,
dreaming of no one, wanting
someone. The moon in the window
throws shadows, fans
like the leaves of the ginkgo tree.

This is a different kind of wanting,
not anguish, not need—
it's suddenly pure
desire.

34

The first ring of ice on the lake
makes the sound of bells
as it breaks. *Ice bells*, I say,
wanting words for my
winter happiness. *Ice bells, solstice,
darkness, solace.* Ice bells.
Ginkgoes, again, lift their arms
to the white bell of the sky.

35

A woman tells me of her breakdown
late in the afternoon. *You see
your life one way, then one day
you turn around
and it's totally changed. You
can't go on. Why is it
then? Why that moment
and no other? Like the moment
the ginkgo lets
all of its leaves go at once.*

36

Sitting in the steamy Lotus,
I read my fortune: *Friends long absent
are being returned to you.*
And, yes, I feel them, the migrations
of the spirits, surrounding
my table like a protective
ginkgo grove. Philip, Bente, Zi Ye.
It's time for sitting still,
for hot tea and good fortune: sugar
cookie in the mouth.

37

On my birch writing table—
a blue porcelain jar,
inscribed with moons and birds
and roses, keeps safe
for winter keeping
my ginkgo leaves.
The only thing I pray for:
to be calm.

38

Sometimes I like to sit and read
the encyclopedia:
porcelain, the finest
translucent ceramic material
was invented in China,
refuge of the ginkgo,
but the word is from the Italian
porcellana meaning vulva
which also gave rise
to the word for cowry shell.
Such strength
in silky
fragility! In the shine
of shells, spring
leaves, sex, and clay.

39

I think of the monks of China,
how they tended the ginkgo trees, how
they cared for the lavish, blossoming,
buttery, living
female trees. Dear brothers!
Sensuous, celibate monks!
We are all sexual, all of us, all
of our lives.

40

Snow is falling in the temples of China.

PART IV ■ MIGRATIONS OF THE SPIRITS

"You have set the powers of the four quarters to cross each other. The good road and the road of difficulties you have made to cross; and where they cross, the place is holy."

—BLACK ELK

LISA TALKING: SUMMER STORM, 1983

for N. Scott Momaday

It was hot & we looked out the window & the air was yellow & the
       blue
sky turning green & we ran out the front door before she could
       say
stay in the house, the storm's gonna hit any minute & sure enough
as soon as we got to the yard we heard her yelling
a tornado could blow you away & we yelled back *but it didn't,*
       it didn't
& we kept running across the yard & the sky went from green
to dark blue-green, pine green, thunder color
rolled in with the sound of thunder
the clouds rolling like waves rolling over themselves & the
       catalpa tree
bowed down like a ballerina taking a bow, with her thousand pink
       bouquets
& the lightning split the yellow & green into
silvery light & then—
big, globby drops hit us—soft & warm—not like the fall rain
that pelts & stings but soft, *soft*, & we
were in the street dancing & she
was yelling out over the thunder
get back in here, that lightning almost hit you
& we yelled back *but it didn't, it didn't*
& she yelled again *get out of the street, that car almost hit you*
& we yelled back *but it didn't, it didn't*
& we went on laughing & waving our arms like fools in the rain
which was coming down really hard now, so hard
that when it hit the street, it bounced back up
& the whole street was like a giant fountain
& we were the statues of nymphs & sea turtles & dolphins
       cavorting
in the spray! & then we noticed the gutters
were flooding & we ran over to the curb, walking along it

like it was a river
but Anna—she got in it—I mean
she just lay down in it like she always would & let the
        water
run all over her & so I did that too then
& the water was deep & warm & we lay there a long time
& we knew that she was probably yelling
get out of the street, you'll be swept away
but we couldn't hear her any more & it didn't
sweep us away, it didn't sweep us down the storm sewer, gone
        forever—

it swept over us, around us, the warm deep summer water
it was an ocean of water & we—we
were the islands, the coral reefs, the tropical
isles & the sand settled in our hair
& the muck settled in the sweet caves under our knees
& we watched the blades of grass float by
& the sticks & twigs & the purple & green rings of rainbows
& we looked up & the sky was rolling over us & the water
rushing under us & we knew that we
were the center of the universe

& when the storm was over & we went back in the house
we were covered with a fine silt & she said
what we knew she'd say, she said *it could've swept you away—*
& we said *but it didn't, it didn't, we're alive,*
we're alive & she came over to us then
& she lifted the wings
of maple seeds out of our hair
& sent us up to the shower
without saying another word.

LANDBRIDGE, BRIDGE OF MUSIC/MOON

We're driving Up North, and this trip
we're listening to Bob Dylan at Budokan and the kids

don't know where Budokan is
so I start in on my usual talk, which is: everyone

riding in my car has to answer my Minnesota
history questions, such as, Where are the headwaters of the

Mississippi?   What are the names of the people
who lived here before the white people came?

Today my first question is: *Who wrote this song, Highway 61*
runs right by my baby's door & they groan and say,

No, not that one again, it's Bob Dylan, please
don't keep singing like that.   And so I ask them the second

question, *Name Bob Dylan's hometown* and they yell out *Malibu!*
No, no, I say, *that's where he lives now, where did he live*

when he was a kid?   Silence in the back seat, where
they are busy weaving bracelets out of embroidery thread.

Timidly, a small voice: *Is he from Up North?   That's right,*
I say, exultant as a quiz show host, *I guess you kids*

get to stay in the car today, cause Up North is
where we're going, Up North, where the air

is sweet, up through the Minnesota corn fields, up
through the scraggly pines and the spooky swamps, Up North

to the real woods & deep lakes. The air
is sweet even here, even though we're stuck in traffic

along with the bikers, the cars hauling boats,
the campers, pickups, all of us bumper-to-bumper, heading

for the last weekend of summer, Up North. What could be more
perfect than being stuck in traffic on a sunny day

listening to Bobby sing, *How many roads must a man walk down*
& I think about him when he was a boy, listening

to his radio in the middle of the night, Chicago Blues,
Blues from the Deep South, & I think of him singing in Japan

where even now the audience is cheering before he finishes
the first line *How many roads* & I realize I don't know anything about

Budokan—is it a small town like Hibbing? I wonder if
the men & women driving by me with their fishing gear, camouflage

suits and waders, ever heard of Bob Dylan, or Budokan. I've never
been to Asia. It's hard enough to get the time and money to

go camping one weekend Up North. But when I'm driving north,
Asia never seems very far away—I think about

the first people walking to America from Asia, over the landbridge,
first to Alaska, down the coast, to Montana,

eventually to here. Was that the route?   Nobody knows that or
why Dylan took his path from Hibbing to Malibu. Maybe the First

Americans didn't walk.   Maybe they came in boats settling
in small towns all along the North and South American coasts.

Maybe they traveled in walrus skin boats. Or tule reed boats
like the ones in Montana and Egypt. Boats would be easier

than walking, even with animals. Or maybe they didn't have to
travel at all, maybe they have always been here, first,

in the small towns Up North. In college my friend Sarah said,
The world is made up of small towns. It doesn't matter where we

live, the center is everywhere. She ended up traveling anyway.
My mind travels where it will, daydreaming, driving

too slow. Sometimes I'm scribbling poems
on my legal pad, on the seat next to me. Maybe I should

get a bumper sticker that says, *Honk if you / poetry,*
a change from the bumper stickers with dog heads.

Would the guys in their pickups lay on the horn?
I have to go on faith, that there's room in Minnesota for me

as well as the guys in their camouflage gear—
visitors in this country

of the First Americans, all of us drawn by the
heartbeat of the lakes and woods, the steady beat of the Shore.

The loons have already flown off to their coastal waters
of Louisiana and Texas, but the woodpeckers are still here,

waiting for us, tapping the birch trees on the edge of the beach.
The beavers' tails are growing fat for their winter sleep.

The ground squirrels will invade our camp
tonight, chickering, & my daughter is talking to me

from the back seat again, saying *Mom, listen, Bob Dylan
sends Special Thanks to Moon Kobayashi,*

*Mom, isn't that name cool. Maybe when I change my name,
I'll change it to Moon Kobayashi. Whatever name you need*, I say,

& her words remind me that tomorrow night the moon
will be full. We'll walk through the woods without

flashlights, without fear. We'll walk along a silver beach,
the girls with their bleached-out hair, looking

like giant dandelions, milkweeds, the color of
a white dove in the sand. We'll imagine

peace in our hearts in the world at war. I'll sit down then
by the fire, content to be tracking

night noises, the wind through the birches, the moon
across the water

thinking whatever drifts though my mind.

TOO MUCH GIVE

In yard goods, there's a yardstick nailed down
on the cutting counter, scissors on a string.
Every Ben Franklin is the same, even here
in Two Harbors, a tourist town. The maple floors slant
and give as you walk around, scanning
bolts of material lined up, piled up, some askew.
Beautiful colors, neon cottons, watery silks, pastel
jerseys. Today I find black velvet, gorgeous
for a crazy quilt, feather stitched with
lavender and gold. Now I'm fingering some blue cotton stars—
I'll know from the feel if there's too much give
to be of use. I dig through the remnant bin, scraps
for baby things, 37 cents. It's automatic, this bargain
hunting, goes back to the days over a dozen years now,
when I walked to town three times a week
with the baby in the stroller,
my life predictable as a clock.

Morning walks, afternoon naps.
5:00, the first glass of French Columbard.
In the spring, bouquets of lilies from the yard.
6:00, cooking dinner. Baby down,
time for quilts, and books, stacks of books.
Time to wonder if he'll come home, if he'll
want dinner, if he'll be pissed
because dinner wasn't what
he wanted, *because*... I never got beyond the
because when he started hitting, my fear
held down by the brandy under the sink.
Nothing was better than being a mother.
That's what I said then. I got up every morning
on time, happy to see my baby. The baby
didn't know anything was wrong. That's what I said then.

I ran on schedule, so different from my college
stance—I laughed when I read Ben Franklin's diary, how
he agonized over his daily schedule! Now I
was the one walking to the Ben Franklin
making a schedule work.

That was a long time ago, and here I am
in the Two Harbors Ben Franklin, making an
unscheduled stop. The kids are intently picking out
embroidery thread—purple, kelly green and red.
They're weaving bracelets while riding
in the car. In fact, that's why we stopped,
they ran out of red. I look
across the cottons, see a young woman
holding her baby on her left hip, holding up,
with her right arm, a swatch of cloth with huge red
and white sailboats—red is the best color for
baby quilts—red is the first color they can see.
She's gazing off, imagining a new design.

Everything that happens is supposed to happen:
I'm here today to forgive that girl,
to forgive her for sewing instead of writing,
for staying home when she should've run,
for drinking when she should've
dialed 911. I'm here to forgive her
for making a life of
remnants, for living a life with too much
give. She looks so frail and lonely
over there, the chunky baby laughing on her hip.

MASSAGE

for Cheryl Bates

Her hands move smoothly, the tension is
dissipating, being drawn
away. I pull back from the pain I know
is leaving my right eye. My shoulders groan
when she works them. I let my mind

pass through images and words: *go away tired dog
of the body.* It's so quiet in the room
we can hear the wind in the elms, the geese
in the park. They're honking, wildly
flapping. So noisy, they must be mating.

My arms are light and graceful, my hands
receivers of pleasure, not just tools
for work. There's some desire
to cry
about this pleasure.

I'm in my own thoughts.
Cheryl says, *The new moon!*
Oh, I say, coming back to her presence
vaguely, *is there a new moon today?*

No, she says, *I'm talking about the moon
on you. Here.
The mark
of the Goddess.*

I laugh out loud. Nobody has ever
called my scar a moon.
The raised crescent
across my round bottom.
It's been there so long, over forty years.

A first memory from when I was three, my first
defiance of my mother.
I had to take baths in the kitchen sink
because I refused to take a shower.
Mother put a flat plug in the sink, an empty
mayonnaise jar on top of the plug
to hold it in place.

She told me to sit still.
I didn't want to sit still. I wanted
to swim and dive, to climb up high
like the women in the summer at the city pool.

I made it to the top of the jar.
I balanced, reached my arms to the sky,
naked and slippery as a silvery fish.
You can imagine the rest.
They came running with bedsheets,
there was so much blood.
The glass in the water
was glistening
in crescent-shaped shards.
They threw me in the middle of the sheets, naked,
like Dumbo, falling
down into the firemen's net.

What's funny is
I don't remember the pain. I remember
the anticipation
of climbing, the thrill of the
risk, just before
the dive.
          I don't remember the pain, I
remember contemplating, in that split
second, yes, contemplating
the nature of flying, the welcome
of the waters below.

I remember the lapping of
the waters, the shimmer of the moons,
me, moving, relaxed
and graceful.
          And it is this moment
I know as the true claim
of the Goddess: *pain recedes*
away from us, delight
remains.

TOOTH FRAGMENTS

1

At age 90, my great grandma
Minnie Tennessee, Grandma Anna's mama,
gummed her mashed turnips, announced:
I been looking into
getting me some false teeth
but I just don't know
if I'd get the good out of them.
She allowed herself one luxury:
enough yellow to dye her long
fat braid.

2

For years I nursed along my single
baby tooth, making do,
its permanent mate dormant
in my jaw. Never chewed
apples on the right side
of my mouth. When it finally fell out,
48 years old, my tongue
felt it go. Driving
to a demonstration, I spit it
out into the palm of my left hand.

Oh, little tooth! Milktooth,
puppy tooth, no fairy godmother
will bring you quarters tonight!

3

That baby tooth had hung around
after all the others were long gone—
each one yanked by a

string tied to the doorknob, an excited
little brother on the other side.

When the blood was washed
away, the little rootless thing—
small as a pearl in my hand.
Where did they go—
those baby teeth, sojourners
under the pillows?

4

On a quiz about working class
roots, Question #1: *I have at least one
family member under the age of 50
who has false teeth.*
Question #2: *I have a missing tooth
or partial plate.* Question #3: *Family gatherings
are smoker-friendly.*

5

My mother's generation aspired
to middle class. *Don't call me a
Southerner. I don't want to be associated
with those ignorant people.* But braces, for instance,
they said I could do without.
She's got good teeth. In photographs,
a closed, thin mouth says
I'm afraid to smile for fear my jagged
canines will catch my upper lip: *The werewolf
girl*, my rueful thought. Even with my
education, what class is that?

6

First x-ray of my teeth:
one permanent tooth wedged
sideways in my jawbone. They said
they'd take it out, put me out
with sodium penothol. Truth serum.

Didn't they give that
to spies in the war?

When I woke up, I was terrified, my feet
cold. Terrified I had talked
in my sleep, told
the secret of my dad, and my mom
would do something terrible.
Why didn't they cover my feet?

I woke up to a raw throat,
choked down tears, a red vinyl couch,
the tooth still ensconced in bone.
Stubborn as my tongue.

7

Mary read a book on
making do: everything in it
we have been doing for 25 years
except for living in a house trailer.
*No matter what, you have to take
care of your teeth.*

What is it now
that I'm neglecting to buy?

8

Mother said, *Don't chew
your ice, it's tacky, plus
you'll crack your teeth.*
I was timid: I didn't open
Coke bottles with my teeth. Ice was different.
Reading on my bed in the summer:
Lipton's tea, fresh mint,
fresh-cracked ice.

9

Now my dentist tries to fill the cracks
with white goop to
smooth them on the inside. It's supposed
to last forever. Two months later,
my tongue catches
the cracks. They hurt.
Who can afford to go back?

10

At our soon-to-be-ex-teaching job,
Norita and I make our way to our last workshop,
a workshop on the Four
Learning Styles. We recite other
things that come in fours:
The Four Humors, The Four Body Types, The Four
Directions, The Four Horsemen of the Apocalypse:
we can only come up with
War, Famine, Pestilence. Surely,
we say, the Fourth is
Teeth in Middle Age—the pain,
the dentist, and his bills.

11

If you complain to the dentist about the pain,
he says, *We'll work with it.*
Him and who else?

12

I wanted to keep this teaching job, a real job,
so I could have my *pretax dollars
withheld for medical expenses*. Then I'd
buy me a new tooth. I needed to set aside
$830, the exact cost of a
bridge.

13

It's all about eating. Making sure
it will all go on. Mashed potatoes
don't cause much anxiety. But corn!
Corn on the cob, with its sweet hulls that
stick in the teeth. Fat golden
carrots cleaned under the faucet,
then chomped. Artichoke leaves
that must be scraped
and sucked. Greek olives with their
hidden pits. Norwegian stew, cabbage and
stringy mutton, hidden nuggets of
black peppers. The pleasures
of chewing
anything you damn please.

14

Somehow the orthodontist got paid
for my daughter's braces.
The plaster cast of her childmouth
still in my sewing box, a remembrance.

15

Stunned when he saw the house
I used to own, my friend asked me,
How could you leave security—
for yourself? How to answer?
I had no choice. The day I knew
that I had to leave was the day
I was delivering political leaflets
out in the country. A blue-eyed
wolfhound ran up behind me, sank
his teeth into the flesh
behind my knee. Nobody was home.
The next day the owners said, *No,*
we never got any rabies shots.
Never. This was way out in the country,
militia country. The County Medical Officer,

my husband, refused
to quarantine the dog. Didn't he
care if I lived or died?
No. It wasn't that. He didn't
want to call attention to himself.

What's true
is his shame of me, teeth
marks in my heart.

16

Even during the time of money, a momentary
respite in the middle class, the greatest
pleasures were those I
gathered: asparagus, trout, columbine,
goat milk, cherries from the orchard,
huckleberries from the mountain, sunshine
in the yard.

17

That lack of action by my husband
became the standard
by which all future humiliations
would be measured. Nothing would
ever hurt that bad again.

Much later, I learned about
kindness. The dog's teeth, then,
I thought of fondly,
the first lesson of my instruction:
how to move from the place of pain.

18

For years I told my friends
If I'm found dead, you know
who did it. My teeth would
never have to be used
to identify my body, it would

be in my house, done in
by the respectable
doctor, my husband, his face
easily described as *beautiful, iconic,
and unknowable.* Why is it
the act of battery
elevates the batterer to mystery?
Why is it people deny
the ordinariness of the crime, say
How much passion he must have in his heart.
I suppose he, too, would have *stolidly
endured the wrenching testimony.*

19

My one permanent tooth, the one
that should've grown in but didn't,
is still wedged sideways in my jaw
but all my secrets are out
in the open.
I practice saying *low-income*
aloud, whenever I need to.

20

My only asset, one tooth
capped in gold.

21

My daughter didn't like her stepfather much
but she remembers how, when he
was the Tooth Fairy, he
would leave sweet congratulatory notes
under her pillow with the quarter. How strange
and unpredictable the imprint we leave
in each other's lives.

22

Where did all her baby teeth go?
Did I throw them all away? Why

didn't I save them in some velvet pouch,
in a dresser drawer?   Why didn't I
go out into the garden at full-moon,
cast-sowing them across
the earth, courage
to grow into life?

They're simply gone,
like so much else, unaccounted for.

23
I look at the gap in my mouth
in a new light. A sign of long life,
experience. After all, the Wife of Bath
was considered lusty because of the gap
between her two front teeth.

24
Should I buy a house trailer?
Would I get the good
out of it before I die?

25
I'm not above spending good money
on a little yellow for my hair.

SEARCHING FOR GRANDPA LLOYD

after Odysseus Elytis

Scrapbook:
Me, age 2, sitting in a little wagon
smoking his pipe. My attire:
underpants, a straw hat.

Memory:
I had a headache. Stayed on his lap
for the whole picnic, right there
under that shade tree. He was wearing his Sunday
seersucker suit, smoking his pipe. Laughed
that deep Welsh laugh, dark circles under his eyes.
Relaxation through my muscles, to all my cells.

Scrapbook:
The glider swing at the farm.
Grandpa holding two babies: Dottie, Rosie.
Cousins Mickey & David on either side.
I can see I was happy: sound asleep in the sun.

Dreams:
He said he would get me a Shetland pony
when I turned 12. If he had lived, he would've.
He liked spoiling his girls. In the middle
of the Depression, he got my mom Betty
her circus horse, Trixie.
He would've protected me
from my dad.

Scrapbook:
Grandpa in a dark suit and hat, bending over
at a beach. Grandma Anna's handwriting
in pencil on the back: *Guy in Mexico*
picking up shells for Betty Jane.

Reality:
Killed when his car was hit, at sunset, turning
onto the highway. Eleven years old, I cried for the loss
of the pony, and him. Years later,
for the loss of his protection.

Scrapbook:
Now that I am their age, when I see their youthful
pictures, I want to call them
by their given names: *Guy   Anna*
He's holding their firstborn, baby Katherine.
Anna in her taffeta. I imagine it dark green.
Did she tell me that before she died?
Guy looks at the camera with intense dark eyes.
In the foreground, his legs crossed, casually,
show his cuff, threadbare.

This is not a man ashamed of poverty.
A man not too proud
to hold babies.

Scrapbook:
In the sweetness
of my brothers' faces, his dark eyes, his smile.

Reality:
His memory offers
an arbor of protection.
That early, accurate trusting in my cells.
The gauge to be used, from deep
inside my body: This man is safe.

THE MISSISSIPPI IN SPRING

Walking up the bluffs above the river
there's nothing between him and me and the sky
but the wind, glorious wind.

When we look down, the Mississippi, far below us,
seems more lake than river
with its inlets, creeks, and bays. Floodtime now,
the river's high, moving up into the willows and brush.
Lush waterland, a breeding ground
for herons, mallards, frogs. The vista
so huge—the bluffs on the other side
seem to be a hundred miles away.

Two blue herons come flying by—mates.
They float easily, turning south, then east,
graceful, in sync, scalloping
the sky. They seem to turn
only for the sake of turning. Then they ride
the updrafts, steadily rising, falling,
turning upwards again. At last they head north,
still in tandem, a wingspan apart.

My heart stops at the thought
they're headed for Prairie Island,
seventy-five miles from here. Will they nest
by the invisible radiation?   Will
their eggs break open before their time?
Their young coming out deformed, eyes
bugging crooked, beaks curling back
into their necks?

The day is so beautiful, it seems
nothing dangerous could be close at hand. We're here

on the bluffs above the river, somewhere
between land and sky. I imagine the unseen
poison, then imagine it gone. I imagine beautiful
windmills on the bluffs, here and across
the river, making a clean harvest
of the wind.

The sun is on my face, and the wind.
May it always be strong, the herons rising with it.

PAINTED CANYON REST STOP

for my brother Philip, again

Pink-coral
streaks through the tops of the Badlands
a color your brushes would have lavished
across thick paper. This layering of earth
comes from the Jurassic Era, your beloved dinosaurs.
The ham sandwiches a darker pink
than the land formations around us.
You'd like the contrast too.
Eating ham sandwiches while viewing
the panoramic view. Today you're
your old self again, engaged, loss
becoming presence.

You've been dead now longer than you were alive.
Time changes who you are. Mostly you're
not you, you're my longing, phantom
limb, can't put my finger on what
I lost. When Richard was in the hospital, the proverbial
bag of bones, I took over your gray wool Pendleton
so he could sit on the patio and smoke—
it hardly fit. How could
I forget your skinniness, your size?

Today we listened to Janis across Montana stretch
her voice, flooring it
from a husky growl to a wail
in three seconds flat. I can't remember—
did you die before or after her?
Bless her heart.

And whose other minds are you still wandering through?

That young girl who came to you in the hospital,
a raggedy fur coat over hot pants at 20 below?

The dentist who for no reason
said, years after your death, *What talent,*
an artist, the class clown, what
a waste.

Just last week my daughter
applied for a job—the manager remembered high school, you:
Oh, he was hot, he was so hot.

The community of loss stretches across
the mountains and plains.

I want to tell you
the latest news:

Not too far from here they found huge nests of eggs.
Mayasaurs. Imagine, nests the size of craters.
Now they think the dinosaurs were warm-blooded,
and brightly colored—orange, magenta, pink.
You didn't have to paint them lizard green after all.
The earth, their skin—a matched set.

Old news, still true: All the drugs
have turned out to be drugs.
In A.A., there's a lot of guys now, your age.

This summer, our second cousin finally sober
died of a heart defect on the operating table.
Maybe you know this.

The war news, it still goes on.
I can't keep up with the rock and roll.
Mystery Science Theater 3000—now
that's something
I wish you'd waited for.

Last night I turned down the sound on Voodoo Lounge,
watched Mick strut on TV, held an ice pack
on my knee. You'd be laughing
at how I somatize.

I wonder if you'd laugh too at me wanting a
cheesy throw-away panorama camera.
Which I do.

At home I have a chair for every window.
Lacking mountains, I watch the trees.

Collecting news for you.

WHEN I CLIMBED THE PYRAMID OF THE MOON

When I climbed the Pyramid of the Moon, it looked
exactly the way I'd thought it would look, the view
opening to the four directions, blue waves of
ridges behind the blues I hadn't seen
from the ground. The green fields, with their
cactus red flowers, were still green below me.
I was content. Calm, even. I wouldn't call the feeling
happiness. I didn't have any of that euphoria,
the buzz of my drinking days, the days I needed
to get high to get some distance from despair, to get to
what I thought was normal, average, up and humming, levitated
above the despair which nevertheless
did not disappear: that clear above-the-clouds high
is a state of mind I no longer desire.

When I climbed the Pyramid of the Moon, I didn't want
to get high.   Neither was I in despair,
but I was thinking about despair: all the years
I wanted the world to be what I thought it should be,
wanting the world to be what it wasn't,
leaving me ill at ease. It was difficult
to face the world, when so much of it was pain:
the Vietnamese child on TIME trying to outrun the
napalm eating her up and my baby:
trying to talk, uttering her first words
of despair, *why baby cryin'?*   I was overwhelmed
by the pain I couldn't fix, by wanting
the life I never got, moments of happiness
swallowed up by the relentless
appetite of pain. I decided to match my mind to
the world as it is, not as I want it
to be. I decided to refuse to want anything again.

When I climbed the Pyramid of the Moon, I walked
back and forth slowly to take in the vast
spaciousness of the view which matched the
inside of my mind. It was exactly the way
I expected it to be—the mountain plateau opening
with clear views to the east and south and west and north.
People of all eras have liked a good lookout. Pyramids,
mountaintops, airplanes, chemicals, treehouses.
The people who built this pyramid didn't leave
their names, only carvings of the distant ocean
shells, the divine serpents and wings, and this pyramid,
this lookout on time and space. It lifts you up—
that doesn't mean you feel high. The walk itself
makes you breathless with the
ebb and flow of muscles and blood. The culminating
weight of the stones pushes up the
intensified knowledge of earth beneath you,
keeping you here, close to the sky, connected to ground.

When I climbed the Pyramid of the Moon, it was calming
to discover that it matched my expectations.
What was happening outside my body paralleled
what was going on inside my mind and I did not think of
wanting, or not wanting, I didn't think of happiness or
despair, what I thought of was *congruence.*
The day had started out congruent, driving
by the neo-city, shacks without
electricity or water, poverty horrible
as you'd ever imagine it. The tropical wind rushing
through the green fields was congruent.
It had been congruent to sit at the outdoor café
under the lemon trees, feasting
on mangoes, melons, limes the size of lemons, watching
the parade of the ruling class in
their leathers, tight pants, and Rolex watches,
and it was congruent to hear my dear traveling companion
mutter to the beggars, *Go away, I'm eating*, then
scowl at the rich, *There is no justice.*

When I climbed the Pyramid of the Moon, I was thinking
Congruence is too deep a feeling to be
called happiness. This is acceptance of the world:
no longer longing for what I don't have, no longer
compelled to take in all the available pain.
It's not that there's nothing to look forward to, not
that no more good will happen, it's not
that I won't ever cry again,
not that I will never take action against
injustice: it means that there are no more
surprises. Cruelty is not a surprise and all
the good things—food, friends, sun,
books—they are equivalents of each other,
and when each new, good thing gets here,
I'm not surprised, I simply say, *Now that it's here,*
it's congruent, it suits me,
I want it. Congruence releases desire:
what I've got I want. I want
this green and blue day, I want this
high altitude breathing, my head tipping back
to bask in the sun and clouds. Now that I'm here,
I want to be standing here,
here at the top of the Pyramid of the Moon—opening
to the four directions,
blue upon blue,
the vast spaciousness of mind.

TO BE CONTENT WITH WHAT IS GIVEN

to sit in your car at the wayside rest
watching the seagulls
high over the water
somehow they're backlit   even though
the fog has taken the sun

to be ordinary
to stop and read every sign on the Nature Trail
unashamed of taking this day hike
this easy hike
hard-driving backpackers scorn

to be present to your life
to walk in the green sweetness of the spring woods
feeling your winter stiffness as you walk
mindful yet not minding —
everyone has scars

to be content with what is given
to take in the dusty sun smell on the piney path
new earth released from snow
to say all the names of the wildflowers
knowing they won't stick in your mind tomorrow —
mertensia   bunchberry   blue-eyed grass

to be gentle to yourself
to walk slowly along the creek
watching the sparkle of rocks in water
pink and gold and silver
the rusty color of root beer —
to stand like a cow in the mud

to be open to ordinary pleasures
to watch the fat moon rise
over the lake   over
the cliff where the cliff swallows fly
to accept the gift of not knowing
before you got here
that the moon would be full

MIGRATIONS OF THE SPIRITS

The week we're leaving for the San Diego conference,
there's a ferocious storm in the Pacific,

the paper says it walloped a transport ship—
thousands of Nike tennis shoes have been swept

overboard, carried away
by the Pacific currents and winds.

The day we land, there are sightings
of tennies strewn along the California coast,

250 on one beach. It is expected
that in six months time,

sightings will be reported in Japan,
proving all speculators

correct when they imagine numerous ancient ocean crossings,
all directions, many kinds of boats. I imagine

ancient traffic as we land and as we head out in the taxi,
everybody is wearing tennis shoes! It's the tropics, all right,

people running around half dressed, the palm trees, the flat
gray battleships out on the water.

The birds of paradise we can scarcely afford three of
for special occasions, publication parties and the like,

are growing like weeds right out of the ground
in front of the Coast Guard. Gold sprays in the air.

They are so beautiful I could go home now, satisfied,
but the taxi driver, twelve years on the road from Afghanistan,

asks if we're going to the communications convention,
Why, yes! we say excitedly, *How could you tell we're writers?*

Good, good, he says, *20,000 people at the convention center.*
20,000? We say, in unison,

this is not possible for poets. *Please tell us again...* I refrain
from talking louder to help him understand.

Tele— he says *Tele—*
communications. He speaks as though we are the foreigners.

Oh, we catch his drift, *Telemarketers! No, no,*
we don't know anything about sales, we write poetry.

So he drives us past the people walking by the convention center
in their brand new white tennis shoes, and heads

for our small hotel. As we pass the Café de L'Amité
I see a white hat placed in the window next to a round table—

the summer white, the shiny black bill, the gold brocade,
official sign of empire, of absolute control,

the same hat my dad is holding in the crook of his arm
in the black and white photo from 1943,

his other arm around my mother, in her soft
rayon pants suit, both of them smiling shyly.

It's sunny in the picture, on the porch of
their first home, here, on the destroyer base.

In the photo I can't see any of the cruelty with which he will
damage all of us, nor the strength with which

she will resist. There is only tenderness
here in San Diego, where I now recall that rayon

comes from a tropical tree, where even now we are crossing
the Coronado Bridge, crossing blue water spreading beneath us,

where the ships look as harmless as my brothers' toys.
In this blue air it is difficult to believe

that anything can be destroyed. At the beach
I'll run barefoot in the sand, pay homage

to the green and turquoise waves. I'll give thanks to
the spirits that brought me here, say

what a good place to be conceived, scan
the waves for what will wash up next—

broken shells, rings of plastic, random white Nikes,
touching base on their way to Japan, on the move—

on this ancient ocean, this ancient beauty, this
ancient buoyancy.

NOTES

Page 9:   for Deborah Keenan who said, *Write a poem with your favorite nouns* and for Lucille Clifton who wrote the poem "speaking of loss."
    Locusts is the word used for cicadas in the Southern United States.

Page 11: The Thich Nhat Hahn quote is from *The Raft Is Not the Shore,* Boston: Beacon Press, 1975.

Page 13: On January 15/16, 1991, the birthday of Martin Luther King, Jr., President Bush announced that the U.S. had bombed Baghdad, Iraq.

Page 15: Judith Lewis Herman, M.D., is the author of *Trauma and Recovery,* U.S.A.: Basic Books, HarperCollins, 1992.
    The quote from Tim O'Brien is from "How to Tell a War Story," *The Things They Carried*, U.S.A.: Penguin, 1990.

Page 26: On All Saints Day it is customary in some churches to stand up for the dead and call out their names. The title of this poem is from the Call to Worship at Lyndale Congregational Church, November 5, 1989, when the murdered women were remembered. "We are surrounded this morning by a great cloud of witnesses. We gather to remember and name and celebrate the lives of family and friends who have gone before us." This call was inspired by Hebrews 12:1: "Wherefore seeing we also are compassed about with so great a cloud of witnesses, let us lay aside every weight, and the sin which doth so easily beset us, and let us run with patience the race that is set before us."

Page 30: *All the whys dissolve into mystery* is from a newspaper article by Al Sicherman about the death of his young son.

Page 35: The Mary Oliver quote is from "The Summer Day," *House of Light,* Boston: Beacon Press, 1990.

Page 38: *Joik* refers to the songs of the indigenous people of Northern Scandinavia, the Sami.

Page 42-43: The Norwegian word *dufte* means *to emit a fragrance.* The quotes are from the poems of Gustav Fröding: The first quote: *For my beloved comes before all the others in this land* is from the poem "En hög visa," a "high song" in reference to the Song of Solomon, which first appeared in *Gitarr och dragharmonika, Guitar and Concertina,* 1891. The second quote: *Tra,la, little sweet nose* is from the poem "Ett gammalt bergtroll," an old mountain troll, which first appeared in *Stäng och Flikar, Odds and Ends,* 1896.

Page 47: The concept of the floating world, *ukiyo,* comes from Japan and refers to the way of living in the world, in the moment, originating in Buddhism. *Ukiyo-e,* pictures of the floating world, was a form of print-making, and continues to be a strong influence in the graphic arts.

Page 51: The correct answers to the riddles on this page are: Smurfette and Martin Luther King, Jr.

Page 55: The Ashbery quote is a complete haiku, second in the series titled "Thirty-seven Haiku," in *A Wave,* New York: Penguin Books, 1985.

Page 57: People respond to this poem with stories of the ginkgo trees they have seen; people have sent me letters with descriptions of the places they have visited ginkgo trees all around the world.

Page 67: The Black Elk quote is from *Black Elk Speaks: Being the Life Story of a Holy Man of the Oglala Sioux,* by Black Elk as told through John G. Neihardt, Lincoln, Nebraska: University of Nebraska Press, 1932, 1988.

Page 69: This poem was inspired by "The Delight Song of Tsoai-Talee," by N. Scott Momaday.

Page 71: Budokan is not a town; it is a large concert hall in Tokyo, Japan. The album *Bob Dylan at Budokan* was recorded at Budokan in 1978.

Page 77: *Send away old dog of the body* is a line from the poem "A Summer Prayer" by John Brandi.

Page 81: QUIZ: written by Mary Frances Platt, published in *Sojourner,* January, 1994.

Page 86: The phrase *beautiful, iconic, and unknowable* was used by writer Richard Corliss to describe Orenthal James Simpson, TIME MAGAZINE, July 15, 1994. *Simpson stolidly endured a week of often wrenching testimony* was a photo caption in the same issue.

Page 90: Prairie Island is the site of a nuclear power plant which is now storing nuclear waste in steels casks on land next to the Mississippi and next to a reservation where Dakota people live.

Page 95: The Pyramid of the Moon is located in Teotihuacan outside Mexico City.

Roseann Lloyd's first collection of poetry, *Tap Dancing for Big Mom,* New Rivers Press, 1986, is now in its second printing. She has also published other books. With Richard Solly, she wrote *JourneyNotes: Writing for Recovery and Spiritual Growth* (Ballentine 1992). She co-translated the Norwegian novel, *The House with the Blind Glass Windows*, by Herbjörg Wassmo, published by Seal Press, second printing, 1995. With Deborah Keenan, she edited *Looking for Home: Women Writing about Exile* (Milkweed Editions) which received an American Book Award from the Before Columbus Foundation, 1991.

Her more recent work can be found in anthologies such as *The Party Train: A Collection of North American Prose Poetry,* New Rivers Press, 1996, and *She Who Is Lost Is Remembered: Healing from Incest Through Creativity*, from Seal Press.

She has received Poetry Fellowships from the Minnesota State Arts Board and the Loft-McKnight Awards. In 1991 Nikki Giovanni chose her manuscript along with Deborah Keenan's for the Loft-McKnight Award of Distinction in Poetry.

Roseann Lloyd was born in Springfield, Missouri, and currently lives in St. Paul, Minnesota.